LABYRINTH OF THOUGHTS

Her garden of words in prose and poetry

Nikka Dominguez

ARPress
ILLUMINATING IDEAS
EMPOWERING VOICES

ARPress
45 Dan Road Suite 5
Canton MA 02021
Hotline: 1(888) 821 0229
Fax: 1(508) 545 7580

Ordering Information:
Quantity sales. Special discounts are available on quantity purchases by corporations, associations, and others. For details, contact the publisher at the address above.

Printed in the United States of America.

ISBN 13:   Paperback   979-8-89389-005-1
           eBook   979-8-89389-006-8

Library of Congress Control Number: 2024906118

Labyrinth of Thoughts are random words molded into sentences and formed into a poem. These are random thoughts of a wandering teenage girl, trying to weigh the pros and cons of life and also knowing the rules of love and pain. A compilation of her poems, some were written at the back portion of her favorite book and others were written in her notebook during her Math class. Every poem is her way of expressing herself or for other people's feelings or experiences. A sneak peek of her artistic mind.

I hope you enjoy reading this book.

Love,

Nikka xx

To Calum Thomas Hood,

You inspire me

un

You

I started writing again because of you.

—Nikka Dominguez

deux

False Hope

Now I know how it feels to
be broken.
The worst part is, that you
don't even know
—how I really feel towards you
You thought that I was just
messing around
well at first, I am
But things do change
It evolved into something
difficult
And hard to understand
is this love or plainly
infatuated by you ?

Acting crazy or even weird,
looking cool,
sometimes we're
unpredictable
But those times that I'm with
you I feel like I am myself
Everything was like a bliss of
a moment
I used to keep my emotions
at bay

But to you—

I am different when I'm

with you

Should I tell you how I feel
towards you?
or should I leave it just like
that?

Don't know what to do now
Seeing you with someone
else makes me feel
like I'm just nothing to you

I can't blame you, there
wasn't so-called "Us" after
all
You've only considered me as
a 'friend'

But for me—

You mean more than that

Everything will now stay as
a memory.
A keepsake of you and me.
My feelings will always stay
as a mystery
I will wait—

Wait until my feelings will

fade

Will fade into nothingness
I think I had enough of your
act,
enough of ~~you.~~
enough of everything!

I can't let go that easily
You became part of my life
And now, you left a hole in
it
A minute we were building a
love that is against all odds
And a minute we were
falling apart

*Thank you for breaking my
heart.*

—Nikka Dominguez

troi

Distant

He left
No words needed to be uttered
No second chances
Nor second awkward; unsteady glances
Just sad smiles were shared.

—Nikka Dominguez

quatre

Happy

I was
I wish to be
I thought I'll be
and hopefully, you would be.

—Nikka Dominguez

cing

Strange Girl

—for Cassandra

A hair like Nimbus clouds
I always knew you hate
someone being loud
Derps and potatoes
Little shoes, hiding your little
toes

In a slippery staircase
Tip-toeing in a quiet pace
A smile written all over your
face
Little moments we can't
erase

You hate being clingy
Yet you love your boyfie
Even when he goes all so
cheesy
But we both adore Halsey

Your unique choices of
songs
Telling me the difference
between right and wrongs
In a place where we felt like
we don't belong

We've got no choice but to
get along

An almost mile walk
It's ok since you're the one
to talk
Your weird remarkable jokes
We laugh so hard until we
choke

Cutie little curls
With my fingers I like to
twirl
You always dream of flying
to New York
Underage, yet we planned on
doing some part time
work

Complaining about your
pimples
You even hate my dimples
Gestures, that makes you
weird and simple
In the eyes of God, ***you're
always beautiful***

A new-found friend
Clicking letters on the
keyboard, until you hit send
I almost faint, my life's over
I want it to end
A good listener, but you
always have time for me to
lend

Your face oh so pale
Waiting for sweatshirts to go
on sale
Attentive in class, never
want to fail
Like Moana, in the wide
ocean your ship sail

Troubling with insomnia
We want to explore Canada
Or maybe a road trip in
California

Stargazing out of nowhere
just listening to Regina

Similar goals
Similar dreams
We share a lot of things
Don't know why, but you're
like a twin in disguise

Hope your relationship stays
strong
Our friendship last long
Don't want this poem to
prolong
My little Nimbus, so long.

—Nikka Dominguez

six

Sunset

So, let me write
the constellations
in the palm of
your hands
Let us seize this
unspeakable moments
And I'll let you
sit beside me
in a place
where sunset sets,
as we'll watch it
go down
right before
our eyes.

—Nikka Dominguez

sept

Lover

You are more than a poem
As you sang lyrics of my favorite song
Being with you felt like home
Wishing you're always be with me
and never be gone

I can't help myself
from laughing; smiling
It felt like it was just you and me
Just us
In this dead night
our lost souls
found each other

I wish to get to know you more
Savoring all my remaining hour
You, as my knight in shining armor
This is my last goodbye, mi amor.

—Nikka Dominguez

huit

The rain

Series of passersby
Walking in the midst of
this lonely street
The warm look of Tuesday afternoon
Sweat of despair
Trickling down like water falls
In the temple of their heads
And down to their jaws.

What came next?
Is something they didn't expect
A cold gust of wind
Slapped their faces
And a numerous grain like rain water
Giving them no time
To open up their umbrellas

Scattered like a swarm of bees in a hive
Looking for a place to hide
A shelter to their now, cold bodies
The pavement reeked with asphalt and
The earthly smell of a wet road
Look how sad everything turned out.

—Nikka Dominguez

Unfinished Poem of a Poet

How the universe of us
collide right in front of
these
million dancing fairy lights
How your eyes fired up
with every beat of these
banging drums of our hearts

How aesthetic old pop
alternative songs, sound as
it left in our mouths
How we let our feet
carries us to the unknown
wild places
How our fingers brushed
with every
breathtaking friction of our
warm being

How the streetlight
illuminates
the side of your left pretty
face
How your smile
tighten the knots in my
stomach
How time passes quickly

as we spent every penny of
our seconds
to the untold stories of our
lives

How it breaks, not just my
heart
but yours as well, to say
goodbye
and end our unpredictable
night
so you said "I'll see you
soon" instead

As I watched you turned
your back
walking; back to the place
you call your 'home'
Wishing you felt at 'home'
with me

As I lie awake
in the comfort of my warm
bed
I remember you.

How you made my night
special and more than
amazing
Replaying all those fleeting
moments with you
No camera could capture
that perfectly imperfect
picture
No words could contain that
every poetic moment we
both shared

No colors could paint that
beautiful art within you.
—and I'm glad I met you.
This poem will remain
unfinished,
unwritten; unpublished

Not until you let me to
Not until you ask me to
Not until our path crosses
again
Not until our lines are
connected again

I know there will be another
right time, for us to meet
and rekindle the sparks of
our eyes
So I'll not end this with
another period
for there will be so much
more to be told
As we'll let the history of
us unfold

*You were a definition of
history and a poetry, indeed*

—Nikka Dominguez

dix

Getaway

Riding up till I lost my way
Follow me right up to the
Milky Way
Much to my dismay
We're better off to part this
way

Moon is high up above
Lonely from being unloved
Quiet empty streets
In that alley we're supposed
to meet

As the wind caress my face
Unsolved questions,
incomplete phrase
Been straining my mind for
these past few days

Passing through these
puddles of rain
Can't seems to ease the
pain
We don't need to feign

Taste the lime of freedom
and break off the chain
As I stepped away and left
words unsaid
Memories tucked underneath
my bed
When I knew you love
someone instead
But I'm not here to beg
Hoping you'd take back the
words you said

Too young to die
Too innocent to lie
Live your life like you
wanted to
Mind your limits as you bid
everyone adieu

—Nikka Dominguez

onze

To Us and From the Lost Me

In lambent lights
Ina place where we're out of sight
Uttering inimitable words
Sang sweetly along with your guitar cords

As another chapter unfolds
Yet our love story remains untold
It was freezing cold
And you wrapped your arms around me, to hold

It was indeed a perfect moment
Hoping we could make this permanent
Everything was spontaneous
And it almost made me suspicious

Two hearts seeking for happiness
Trying to break the chain of loneliness
Until a shot of liberty was felt
That made the two hearts melt

—Nikka Dominguez

douze

Bookmark

Do you ever think about
What's between these chapter
of the book of ours?
Pages that you've marked red
Torn and crumpled
What if we're only a short story
and not a mere series
What if 'us' is not an essay
but only a mere sentence
that ended with a period
An understatement
Even though, I thought
It is us against the world
When it is only me against us
Sadly, I gave my heart
only to the wrong man
Now, I think I shouldn't give a damn
Screw this rhyme

—Nikka Dominguez

treize

Smitten

Unexpected smiles and deadpan humor
Wearing a plain white color
Awkward glances and weird beating of heart

Saw you standing at the end of the hallway
Tongue tied and I don't know what to say

I was running off to my next class
And my heart was pounding so fast
You were there as I approached the gate
And I end up smiling even if I was already late

Your warm personality
Your approach with heartfelt sincerity
Keeps on denying this feeling
I'm just tired of trying

Chances were odd
And all I gave you was a nod
I should've grabbed the opportunity to say 'Hi'
Once again, I want to see you smile.

—Nikka Dominguez

quatorze

Queen

You're an uncrowned majesty yet you deserve a diamond—made
chaplet
You wore your red lipstick as splendid the way as Juliet Capulet
I was there during your downfall like a leaf during autumn
season
The rocks you stumbled upon
makes you a fighter in our 'strong independent woman' generation
You and I have this invisible connection
We always got ourselves stuck in a different kind of weird
imagination
But do you remember when we always got each other's back for
motivation?
I would let you read all my made up poems and quotes for
inspiration.
I love how your eyes twinkled with amazement
Every time we shared a beautiful kind of sentiment
You always adore the city lights
We even dreamed of flying to random places to witness those
breathtaking sights
I'd always love the brown pools of your eyes
How it glint with surprise
how happiness reaches the deepest corners
I'd always love to see you smiling
You, warm people's heart with your humorous way of talking
A day would be boring if you weren't around
For— you glow like a midnight sun in a moonless sky

—Nikka Dominguez

quinze

Half a Heart

How can she love that hard?
When half of her heart
Still belongs to the man
She used to love?

—Nikka Dominguez

Never Be

The moon rises up in the
lonely sky
With a glint of surprise in
my blurry eyes
A little wish from a crying
soul
That maybe someday you'll
going to hear my call

Trying to recall all the
memories we had
How I really wish to bring it
back
When a flower starts to
bloom
But literally dies at the end
of the day
When a clock starts to tick
And the world starts to
reverse
A tear starts to drop from
the corner of my eye

My mind was crowded with
thoughts
Those what if's and maybe's
Would I ever make it 'till
the end of this Journey?
If today I don't have any
company
The dawn is now appearing

And the shadows are
deceiving
The sparkling precious ring
in my hand
Clutching it closer to my
heart

Thinking why you have to
go away
Because you promised that
you're here to stay
Baffled with different
conclusion
Tell me is there any
solution?

Feeling anxious, and asking
myself
"Am I too ambitious?"
I want to leave it all behind
With another place to find
Maybe I'm just too blind

Time travels so fast
And I know this won't last
As my love for you turns to
dust
Inside my pocket is a
hidden knife
And I know this could take
away my life

With just a blink of an eye,
In the sand, my body coldly lies
Farewell as I may go, don't worry my love I'll wait for you.

—Nikka Dominguez

dix-sept

Untamed

I felt sad
Knowing I was just a passerby
in your love story
Not a bystander
but just a mere stranger

hoping to receive the
same spotlight given
to the female lead character
hoping to be part of the show
I was built to strengthen
the bond between
the two

where I stand as the
villain
—the one who steals, hurt and usually dies
The role was never given to me
I made it
I let myself get involved into it
and now I end up suffering
from the thrill of it.

"Cut the scene
cut your skin
Put on your masks
I shall shut the one who asks
I'll tiptoe inside
let's see who will survive."

Maybe that's what they want me to be
to be an evil witch

But then I'm not
As what I've said
I was just a passerby
who happened to step into
other people's story book

Just a mere writer
who happened to scan someone else's work
Just a mere villager
who happened to fall in love with somebody else's king

So, who shall I blame?
My heart who only beats to the one she loves
or
My brain who refuses to function when he's around

I was just the plot twist
they wish that never happened
I should've just closed my eyes and pretend that it never
happened

and close the book
of the love story
that I've never written
So, I'll ripped the pages of our memories
and let it burn along with the words you said to me.
Let me say goodbye

as I felt the 'fighter' in me, died inside.
—for You're clearly not the war I was destined to fight for.

—Nikka Dominguez

dix-huit

Uncovered

You said that you like
the constellations of stars
So I build a whole new Galaxy in me

You said you can't decide which color
So I painted a rainbow in my bedroom door

You don't like it when someone cries
So I turned my back and put up a huge smile

You said daisies are beautiful
So I lay myself in a garden of flowers

You want to be just like Superman
So I dressed up like Lois Lane

You said you want to know what lies beyond the horizon
So I sailed and realized that it was all work of fiction

You said you like the metaphor in my poems
So I made a book out of it instead

But you said you like her
So I laugh
then looked away and said "I know"

—Nikka Dominguez

dix-neuf

True

A true heart that loves
Always forgive
And
Not the other way around

—Nikka Dominguez

vingt

Parting

Writing down these words
sheets of plain, crumpled papers
Hot tears rolling down

Cannot bear to see
Suffering along with me
I made up my mind

I will leave you these words
'We're done, I'm tired'
Unsaid, scars left unopened
Letting my heart break

Unfulfilled promise
Sorry for not saving 'Us'
Believe me,
I tried.

—Nikka Dominguez

vingt et un

To Write About You Seconds after You Left Is

—Inspired by Sarah Kay's 'To Write about You after You

Are Gone Is'

To lie awake in the midst of the night's darkness
The freezing loneliness
of being left alone in the mattress
To wait until September
And wake me up when it ends.
The Goosebumps on my arms
From the memory of your
Calloused fingers clutching me
Closer to your warmth
—and away from harm

To find Gazania boasting its brilliant colors
In shades of yellow and orange
As you left them, with a note
And a bittersweet chocolate
Arranging them in a bundle

Watching them explode
Exquisitely inside my room
And then— to wait until
they have wilted, died, crumpled and been cleared,
No signs of 'what's used to be there'
But just a mere empty and broken vase.

To shout at the woman in the mirror,
To blame her all the misfortunes
The rain, the wood burning in the fireplace
The feeling of being slapped across the face
The realization of—
'the man you love walked away'
Knowing no amount of tears
Can take back all those years
Knowing no one can heal
And his promises that could kill

Knowing no one knows what you feel
As I climbed back to bed
All those fleeting moments we had
Will be a keepsake of you and me
As there was once called 'us' In our made-up fantasy

—Nikka Dominguez

vingt-deux

Ode to My Phantom Lover

You glided across
In my train of thoughts
A knight in my dream
Saving me from my own insanity
In this world full of profanities
You wore a plain white tee
And a black skinny jean
You inherit DiCaprio's genes
Riding a black hummer
You are my favorite kind of summer
Warm and colorful
Enough to make my heart melt
And my eyelashes flutter
Clutching my hands
Entwined between your delicate fingers
Listening to the melancholy tune
Of the midnight breeze
We are lost in our own euphoric state
My getaway drugs
Hopelessly in love between
Nightmare and lost dream

—Nikka Dominguez

vingt-trois

Subject

I asked you before
'Will be my subject for my poems?'
And you said, 'yes'
But never in my wildest imagination
That I'll end up writing a whole book out of it.

—Nikka Dominguez

vingt-quatre

I am Yesterday

You walked past me
Averted your gaze away
No trace of recognition
Our numerous somber
encounters
Now, I'm just another fish
In this sea of strangers

You are my starless sky
No more thousands of
gleaming lights
That dances before my eyes
You were my favorite flavor
of the day
You were my definition
Of the spring month of May

I am no longer a part of
your future
but just a mere memory,
Like a lesson in Geometry,
easily forgotten.
Our love like bundle of
flowers,
wilted and now rotten.

I am now just one of your
few
One of the people that you
once knew
Whispering secrets in the
corridors
Our history tucked behind
closed doors
No more pretty shades of
warm colors
Of your eyes that I always
adore

So, I closed the book of '
Ours'
Ripped the letters of 'Us'
Burned the Memory of 'You'
And mended the shards
Of my broken heart once
more.

—Nikka Dominguez

vingt-cinq

Abandon

You are a combination of love and agony
That I've come to endure
Until it consumed me for good
We carefully stood
To the stage of tomorrow
But you made a step back
Saying you're not yet ready
Thinking, maybe it was because of me
Confusion takes over
As I saw you
Surrender your heart
To another

—Nikka Dominguez

vingt-six

Midnight Lullaby

Her thoughts left her again
traveling to places; to you.
She found herself staring at the rain
dropping carelessly at her window pane

A glass of chilled alcoholic drink in her right hand
one for loneliness
two for emptiness
While her left, brushing a tear that's threatening to fall.

A throbbing sensation in her skull
Making her, once gleaming eyes into dull
Her life didn't turn out to what she planned for
So she drank her sadness once more.

—Nikka Dominguez

vingt-sept

Befriend

I was holding a pen of memories
looking at the blank white pages
I struggled in trying to reminisce the memory of the old you
Clicking tongues as I smiled at the thought of what we used to
do
We used to hangout before
But 'that' stopped when I told you that you're the one I adore
I should've just let it go and just go with the flow
In that way, I could still be your friend even if it's just for a
show

—Nikka Dominguez

vingt-huit

Call

A vibration of my phone
A familiar name registered
Someone called for a late night talk
I thought nothing too serious
But then his tone fading; becoming mysterious
The history that lies before us
A long lost feeling
finally settling in

In the quiet room; I tip toed outside
Hearing his voice
after a month that felt like years
Emotions bottled up like unrolled tears
Catching up with every penny of time that we've lost
Talking as if every single second cost
I heard he was doing fine; but then they were wrong
He clearly wasn't
I knew; the very moment he muttered a clipped word 'Hi'
And with his every

sentences that ended up with a sigh
After sometime I ended up the call and typed
"Tell me what happened, I'll be here for you; but can't hear
you though."
He replied and then it goes on and on,
Until we decided to call it a night
Behind those text messages
is a boy with a broken wings
from a broken home; a messed up life
that night
I felt his sadness; his emptiness

his longing
his battle cry
of the war inside him
And my heart ached for him
So I prayed for him; that's what he needed.

—**Nikka Dominguez**

vingt-neuf

To the Wild

We'll finally meet
in random cities
where we've never
been before
We'll finally meet
where no one will
recognize us
One of us flies,
the other brings a car
and in it we set out
for some destinations
a planned getaway
We'll go to the unreal places
that always appear
in our dreams
The road
stretches endlessly ahead
and behind us
so that we are out of time
as well as out of place
the bond between us
will always be
treasured and remembered

—Nikka Dominguez

trente

Placidity

You were silently observing the flock
Laughing along to those silly jokes
Maybe you're trying to open up your heart's lock
We're like —masking our sadness kind of folks

You always make the conversations lively
Adrenaline rushing unexpectedly
As we'd ride off to the best night of our lives
Wind gushing, chilling our vibes

Silhouette of a big man's figure
Eerie stillness of the night's air
A baffled young mind of yours— quite unsure
As you puffed circles of smoke; filling your lungs with warm
pleasure.

Calmness envelopes your being
A sense of being alone; left your thoughts
As you scurried away; back to us—people you call your 'friends'
A home; not a place but people.

—Nikka Dominguez

trente et un

Prey

Taunting eyes and a predator-like glances
She is like a wild cat lost in this deep forest
So feisty yet so vulnerable
Like a cub wearing her mother's crown

So I tried stealing quick glances,
maybe I could get some chances
So I wore my crown, for her to know
that I'm the king of this lost town

I found myself walking towards her path
Without breaking the eye contact
She was looking at me with admiration
As we both know we finally found each other.

—Nikka Dominguez

trente-deux

Friday

So we are both tangled
by the red thin strings
of our messed up thoughts
Our fingers finally
fitting in to the puzzles of our hands
Walk with me
to the long road of sentiments
And I will look up to your
towering height
What a beautiful sight,
Then you would tell me
how you hate the warm sun
how you hate sadness
And I started to think deeper
To weigh all the wrongs and proper
You made my mind works
Our happiness bursting like fireworks
The unsweetened coffee day
old songs and random talks;
ticking clock
"I have 30 minutes left"
Comfortable silence kicking in
just the sound of the busy streets
and people mingling
We'll look forward to another day
A man of more than a poetic line, indeed.

—Nikka Dominguez

trente-trois

Holidays

You showed me the way
We're mimicking each other's stride
Leaning side by side
Two castaways
of this lonely galaxy of nothingness

It was a long road
with stop signs and U-turns
No pedestrian lanes
thinking, maybe it was because they don't want people getting
on our way

No streetlights
thinking, maybe it was because he brought me sunshine
While I'm hiding and wrapping myself with box of darkness

It was a long road
of sentiments and fondness
No stage acts
Just plain familiarity towards each other's company

No dull milliseconds
A well wasted minutes
of comfortable silence
A staring competition
Of retinas and irises

But you changed your destination
No longer heading to the place we call 'home'
I can't bail myself out
I end up missing out

You showed me the way
But you brought the torch of light and happiness with you
I've got no audacity to walk forward
As I stare at you, withdrawing yourself
slowly stepping backward

So I stayed, standing awkwardly amidst of this odd space
Just right where we lost it.

—Nikka Dominguez

trente-quatre

Subtle

Yellow street lights that blinded her senses
Her directions were undecided
There she goes unnoticed
Maybe she was seeking for comfort
—sadly with the wrong crowd
She walks with pride but no longer proud
Not hearing any sound
She crossed the street
People she was supposed to meet
But something strange caught her attention
Herself— lying coldly wrapped in a cotton sheet
Eyes open but no longer breathing
Blood scattered like roses in Valentine's day
This is where she finally ends her day
She smiled
Painless; finally free.

—Nikka Dominguez

trente-cinq

Damnation

dull boring painted walls
Silent lifeless hallway
Weary bloodshot eyes
dry chapped lips
Others are patiently waiting
Others were busy trying to look for their way in
I saw dust
I saw rust
I saw smiles
others are faint cries
Struggling yet fighting
I saw life
I saw a sharp knife
I saw death
As I finally saw how you take away
that man's last breath

—Nikka Dominguez

Once

Look at that breathtaking
 scenery
A woman lost at sea
Drowning from its own misery
Grasping for sanity

You feel how fast her heart beats?
That's the sound of defeat
She saw her reflection in the water
Nothing but a face for worldly pleasure

The ruined innocence
of a young girl's memory
A story that you never anticipated
nor you expected

Digging through boxes of hidden treasures
Not any golds or diamonds to share
but dark memories of tomorrows
remained tucked; unshared

An estranged man
Leading her into an unfamiliar place
Poor thing, didn't know
what that man might bring

Next thing she knew,
She was locked behind the door
Hands trapping her
Pinning her roughly

Nothing but soft sobs can be heard
In that enclosed space
Until a shot of escape
She grab that chance and ran
far and away from that man

It left her drained
tears dried up; hands shaking
A stranger's kiss remained
haunting her soul, her innocence; her childhood
Even if she bathed herself
with scorching pool of hot water
She even painted her body with glowing colors
And wore hundreds of handmade masks

It is unfair
So young to know the cruelty of life
So young to witness this madness
So young to be filled with sadness

She can't rewrite her past
So she focused herself on what lies ahead
The scars are still there
But she chose to forgive

She cried herself a story
And wrote it down in a paper, stained with tears
Letting her sorrows sink in
Her life, like puzzles finally fitting in

—**Nikka Dominguez**

trente-sept

End

Missed calls and unseen messages
Tell me are we going to end this?
Don't know what to do.
But all I want is you.

Waking up at three
Tell me, do I still make you happy?
It was all my fault, I'm sorry.

Closed doors and awkward spaces
Where are the smiles I used to see in our faces?
I've got nothing but these broken pieces.

Don't know how to end this piece
Love I'm sorry, all I want is peace.
Sad eyes and sad smiles.

Staring out of nowhere
Cold hands and silent tears
I'm not used to it
But I'm trying to reach you out
And settle us up.

Words no longer rhymes.
Hollow mind and messed up ideas.
So, I will end this, but not us.

—Nikka Dominguez

Pendulum

He lay motionless
Fresh tears cascading like
waterfalls
On the side of his cheeks
Eyes glued to the ceiling
But his mind was traveling
From loops of time and
memories
He walks clueless
From the lines of truth
And the dead end of being
a youth
He lived freely
But with the aid of knowing
his limits
And acknowledging his worth
He was swimming back and
forth
Like a dead fish
He's letting himself go with
the river's flow

Seeking for inner peace
Drove by to the nearest cliff
Putting his self at ease
As the clock strikes twelve
A man hangs himself
Smiling at the wicked show
He's a lonely man
With a madman soul
Leaving no trace
As he disappeared into
space
Trickery to the bold naked
eyes
Ended nothing but just an
old tale
Tell no one, or else he'll
hunt you down
One by one.

—Nikka Dominguez

Gaucherie

I am just one of your few
Like in a thriller movie, you left me with a clue
Now, I'm mending these shards of my broken heart with a glue
Trying to be the person that you all once knew
All my cares flew
To an unplanned rendezvous
Like Cinderella who left her shoe
Like James and Alyssa, I also want to run away with you
But then you weren't true
Casting all my tears and fears away
Packing my things in dismay
You didn't stay and again, I am left with nothing to say
I was so tactless, so clumsy
Too late to say I'm sorry

—Nikka Dominguez

Wondering Wanderer

Friction between the rough surface of the road and the tire
Igniting my soul; Fueling the bonfire
Morning breath of a lone traveler
Genuine smile plastered on its lips

Engrossed in her random little trips
Gentle kisses of 2AM November air
Overlooking the quiet quarter moon
Street lights in colors of yellow and white

What an aesthetic sight, we can drive all night
Looking for the answers in the pouring rain
Though there's no signs of an early cloud's tears
We can long for the lonely sea or stay at home and sip your
tea

You can set the time on your clock but never the time of your
life
You can love and get hurt but why hearts can't easily forgive?
You can run away and get lost with your own world
Everything can be so unpredictable

Search for the voice within
Of the frustrated artist
Of the failed writer
Of the unfinished lover
Of the sinner

Wake up and be renewed
Lift your hand to your heart
And satisfy yourself with God's work of art
Let all the wounds heal

Look for your name in the vast space
And leave no trace of hate and defeat
As you stand on both of your feet
And together we'll look forward
for tomorrow, once more.

—Nikka Dominguez

quarante et un

Spring

You were too plain and
I was too colorful.
Yet we matched like bursting colors
of flowers that blooms in May

—Nikka Dominguez

quarante-deux

Last Night

I had a long late night deep talks with Sofia
We talked about all the things
That we rarely talked about before
It was about
Life
Future
Loneliness
History
And of course, You.

—Nikka Dominguez

quarante-trois

Steps

Again, I found myself walking and retracing
My steps back to you.

—Nikka Dominguez

quarante-quatre

Waves

Listen to the waves
Calm and inviting
Just like you
I want you
Near me
And hear my heart beat
—For it only beats for you.

—Nikka Dominguez

quarante-cinq

Writing

The night air slowly lulling me in
But I clearly remember
Telling her how much I adore you
I remember her telling me
To write again
Not for you
Nor anyone's sake
But for myself
To let the idea of you
Sink into the deepest depths
Of discarded feelings

—Nikka Dominguez

quarante-six

Notes

Write it down
Express it into words
—the pain you're feeling in
The phase you're going through
Let your ideas run wild
Let yourself go with the idea of
'not wanting to write about him'
But write it anyway
Everything about him
And own it
Until your mind gets tired
of remembering moments that
includes about him
Until your hands get tired from
Writing down all the words
That you wanted to tell him
From the very start
And until your heart
Gets tired of trying
To figure out where you went wrong
And what could have been
If he stayed

—Nikka Dominguez

quarante-sept

Walk

Heart pounding, a look of annoyance
Been struggling to keep
My composure at bay
I was again stuck in your trance
My lips parted as you
Held my trembling hands
A tingling spark of
What's used to be there
My pace matching yours
Just to keep you close

—Nikka Dominguez

quarante-huit

Maybe

Maybe it was because of the sun setting
The yellow horizon disappearing
A war between dark and light hues
Of colors in the vast sky

Maybe it was because of the clouds
Covering the sun
That warmness left your lips
And the adoration in your eyes
Did the same too

Coldness engulfs your towering physique
A backdrop of dying stars
Losing its brightness

Maybe it was because of the white stripes
In the pedestrian lane
That my mind refused to think straight
Making me feel light in the head

Taking the opposite path
And slowly walking away
From the people
That's not meant for me

—Nikka Dominguez

quarante-neuf

Start

The warm sun is out
Heading towards south
Sipping a cold coconut drink
So, I'm down writing and wasting
My pen's ink
Filling my system with good music
And feeding my soul with positivity
Never seen such beauty
As the clouds outside
Formed and scattered artfully
A great way to aid loneliness
Rest your heart dear, we'll get through this

—Nikka Dominguez

cinquante

Labyrinth

It wasn't about the rhyming
in her poems
That made her known
But it was the message
behind those letters
For the people she ought to
give her heart away

It wasn't about the pain
But it was about all the
swirling ideas of words
Of poetry she wanted
To let the world know

It wasn't about the love she
wanted to receive
Nor the love she dreamed
of

It wasn't about the guy who
left her
Nor the guy she left behind

It wasn't about her
loneliness
Nor the emptiness in the pit
of her
Scarred heart

It wasn't about the scarcity
of attention
Nor the paucity of self-love

It wasn't about the roses in
her hand
Nor the scripted smile in her
lips
It was her garden of
thoughts
That made her unique
Her own labyrinth

It is about her and how
she can be your sweetest
downfall
If you just let her be

—Nikka Dominguez

About the Author

Nikka Ejercito Dominguez is an eighteenyear-old poetry writer from Philippines. She has a weird adoration of the smell of the piled books in the library. She writes, she read and she paints. A lover of her own self and a dreamer of true love.

www.ingramcontent.com/pod-product-compliance
Lightning Source LLC
Chambersburg PA
CBHW020338130626
46549CB00003B/1212